D0824701

How It Is Made

Wax to Candle

B.J. Best

Cavendish Square

New York

Published in 2017 by Cavendish Square Publishing, LLC
243 5th Avenue, Suite 136, New York, NY 10016

Website: cavendishsq.com

This publication represents the opinions and views of the author based on his or her personal experience, knowledge, and research. The information in this book serves as a general guide only. The author and publisher have used their best efforts in preparing this book and disclaim liability rising directly or indirectly from the use and application of this book.

CPSIA Compliance Information: Batch #CW17CSQ

All websites were available and accurate when this book was sent to press.

Library of Congress Cataloging-in-Publication Data

Names: Best, B. J., 1976- author.
Title: Wax to candle / B.J. Best.
Description: New York : Cavendish Square Publishing, [2017] | Series: How it is made | Includes index.
Identifiers: LCCN 2016026017 (print) | LCCN 2016026877 (ebook) | ISBN 9781502621184 (pbk.) | ISBN 9781502621191 (6 pack) | ISBN 9781502621207 (library bound) | ISBN 9781502621214 (E-book)
Subjects: LCSH: Candlemaking--Juvenile literature. | Candles--Juvenile literature.
Classification: LCC TT896.5 .B47 2017 (print) | LCC TT896.5 (ebook) | DDC 745.593/32--dc23
LC record available at https://lccn.loc.gov/2016026017

Editorial Director: David McNamara
Copy Editor: Rebecca Rohan
Associate Art Director: Amy Greenan
Designer: Alan Sliwinski
Production Assistant: Karol Szymczuk
Photo Research: J8 Media

The photographs in this book are used by permission and through the courtesy of: Cover Sean Pavone/Shutterstock.com (left), Maya Kruchankova/Shutterstock.com (right); p. 5 photo by Szilas in the Nationalmuseum, Stockholm/Matthias Stom/File:Stom - A Young Man Reading at Candlelight.jpg/Wikimedia Commons; p. 7 Audrius Merfeldas/Shutterstock.com; p. 9 Gmhofmann/File:Paraffin.jpg/Wikimedia Commons; p. 11 amphaiwan/Shutterstock.com; p. 13 Yawar Nazir/GettyImages News/Getty Images; p. 15 AP Images/Matthias Schrader; p. 17 Christina-J-Hauri/iStockphoto.com; p. 19 Yawar Nazir/Getty Images News/Getty Images; p. 21 Dorling Kindersley/Getty Images.

Printed in the United States of America

Contents

Candles have been used for 5,000 years.

People used them for light.

Candles are made of wax.

Wax was first made with animal fat.

Wax is also made by honey bees.

Today, wax is made by **refining** oil.

It is called **paraffin** wax.

Candles have a **wick**.

The wick is the part of the candle that burns.

11

A wick is a long string.

It is made of cotton.

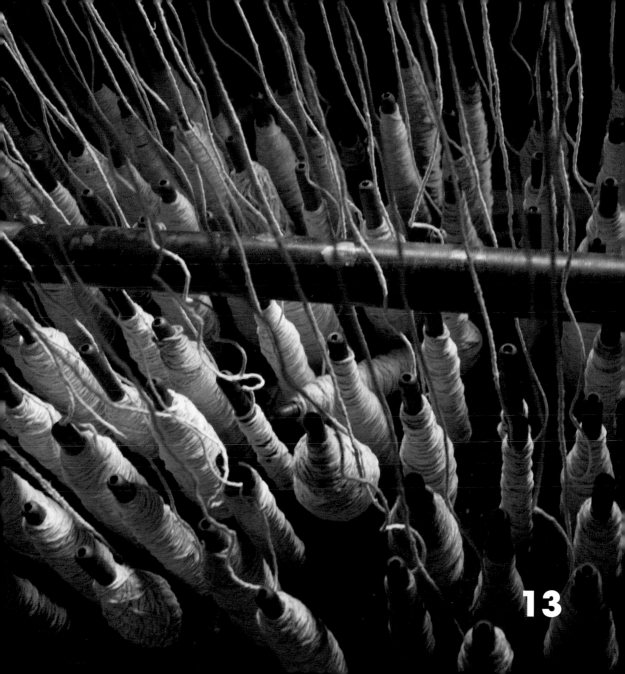

There are a few ways to make candles.

A wick can be dipped in melted wax.

The wax cools.

It becomes hard.

Then the wick is dipped again.

The steps repeat.

17

18

It cools and makes a candle.

Hot wax is poured into the mold.

A wick can be placed in a **mold**.

These are new candles.

They are ready to be lit!

21

New Words

mold (MOLD) A shape where a liquid can be poured.

paraffin (PAIR-uh-fin) Wax made from oil.

refining (ree-FINE-ing) Cleaning oil so it can be used.

wick (WICK) The long string inside a candle.

Index

About the Author

B.J. Best lives in Wisconsin with his wife and son. He has written several other books for children. He has made candles at home.

About

Bookworms help independent readers gain reading confidence through high-frequency words, simple sentences, and strong picture/text support. Each book explores a concept that helps children relate what they read to the world they live in.